M000266716

Dear Friend,

The sweet cooing of a baby is surely the best sound in the world! Making that bundle of joy comfortable & happy is important, and with knitting, it's also fun! These twelve all-new designs to knit are perfect for both novice and experienced knitters. The oh-so-sweet projects include warm blankets, hats and booties, soft washcloths, and squeezable toy farm animals. There's even a cozy cardigan to knit with variegated yarn. Each project is ideal for a shower gift or anytime gift.

Enjoy making these little knitted "hugs" for all the precious babies you know!

Vickie & Jo Ann

LEISURE ARTS, INC.
Little Rock, Arkansas

Blanket,
instructions on page 14

2

Booties,
instructions on page 15

Pamper that darling baby with these sweet gifts! The soft Blanket is quick to knit on the diagonal. Just imagine the cute novelty buttons you could use on the triple-strap Booties!

Variegated yarn creates an interesting pattern on the handsome cabled Cardigan. The adorable Striped Hat is a great way to use any extra yarn you have on hand. With its floppy brim, the Eyelet Cap looks playful!

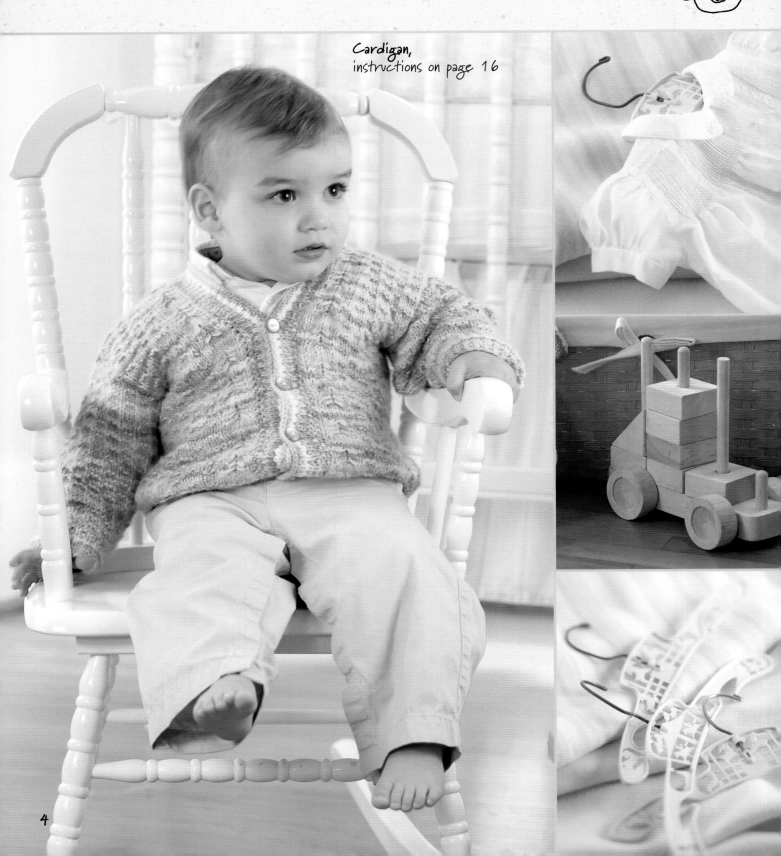

Cardigan,
instructions on page 16

Striped Hat,
instructions on page 22

Eyelet Cap,
instructions on page 24

Whether it's nearing naptime or time for a game of "let's pretend," Baby will love a Blanket with Chick Hood or a Blanket with Pig Hood! They're also fun to wear while listening to favorite fairy tales.

Blanket with Chick Hood,
instructions on page 27

Huggable, squeezable playtime pals are a necessity for every baby. These two knit designs have come from the farm to visit and are happy to spend time with a special little person. They're even dressed for the occasion with polka-dot bows!

Piggie,
instructions on page 28

Both dolls have dimensional ears and noses. The pink Piggie has a curly tail, while the spotted Cow has little knitted horns.

Cow,
instructions on page 32

Turn bath time into fun time just by doing a little knitting? You can! It's easy with these soft & colorful Washcloths with Barn, Tree, and Tractor designs. You can even put tiny red apples on the Tree Washcloth by stitching simple French Knots!

Barn Washcloth, instructions on page 11

Tree Washcloth, instructions on page 13

Tractor Washcloth, instructions on page 12

Barn Washcloth

■■□□ EASY

Shown on page 10.

Finished Size: 7³/₄" (19.5 cm) square

Materials

Medium Weight 100% Cotton Yarn [5 ounces, 236 yards (140 grams, 212 meters) per ball]: One ball
Straight knitting needles, size 7 (4.5 mm) **or** size needed for gauge

Gauge

In Stockinette Stitch, (knit one row, purl one row) 19 sts = 4" (10 cm)

Washcloth

Cast on 37 sts.

Rows 1-7: Knit across.

Row 8: K4, P 29, K4.

Row 9 (Right side): Knit across.

Row 10: K4, P 29, K4.

Rows 11 and 12: Repeat Rows 9 and 10.

Row 13: K8, P 21, K8.

Row 14: K4, P8, K1, P 11, K1, P8, K4.

Row 15: K8, P4, K1, P1, K9, P1, K1, P4, K8.

Row 16: K4, P 10, K1, P7, K1, P 10, K4.

Row 17: K8, P4, K3, P1, K5, P1, K3, P4, K8.

Row 18: K4, P 12, K1, P3, K1, P 12, K4.

Row 19: K8, P4, K5, P1, K1, P1, K5, P4, K8.

Row 20: K4, P 14, K1, P 14, K4.

Row 21: K8, P4, K5, P1, K1, P1, K5, P4, K8.

Row 22: K4, P 12, K1, P3, K1, P 12, K4.

Row 23: K8, P4, K3, P1, K5, P1, K3, P4, K8.

Row 24: K4, P 10, K1, P7, K1, P 10, K4.

Row 25: K8, P4, K1, P1, K9, P1, K1, P4, K8.

Row 26: K4, P8, K1, P 11, K1, P8, K4.

Row 27: K8, P 21, K8.

Row 28 AND ALL WRONG SIDE ROWS THRU Row 50: K4, P 29, K4.

Row 29: K8, P 21, K8.

Row 31: K8, P 21, K8.

Row 33: K8, P8, K5, P8, K8.

Row 35: K8, P8, K5, P8, K8.

Row 37: K9, P7, K5, P7, K9.

Row 39: K 11, P 15, P 11.

Row 41: K 13, P 11, K 13.

Row 43: K 15, P7, K 15.

Row 45: K 17, P3, K 17.

Row 47: K 18, P1, K 18.

Row 49: Knit across.

Rows 51-57: Knit across.

Bind off all sts in **knit.**

Design by Linda Daley.

Tractor Washcloth

■■□□ EASY

Shown on page 10.

Finished Size: 7³/₄" (19.5 cm) square

Materials

Medium Weight
   100% Cotton Yarn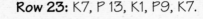
[5 ounces, 236 yards
(140 grams, 212 meters) per ball]:
   One ball
Straight knitting needles, size 7
   (4.5 mm) **or** size needed for gauge

Gauge

In Stockinette Stitch,
(knit one row, purl one row)
   19 sts = 4" (10 cm)

Washcloth

Cast on 37 sts.

Rows 1-7: Knit across.

Row 8 AND ALL WRONG SIDE ROWS THRU Row 50: K4, P 29, K4.

Row 9 (Right side): Knit across.

Row 11: Knit across.

Row 13: K 10, P3, K9, P7, K8.

Row 15: K9, P5, K7, P9, K7.

Row 17: K8, P3, K1, P3, K5, P 11, K6.

Row 19: K6, P2, K1, P5, K1, P4, K1, P3, K4, P4, K6.

Row 21: K6, (P3, K1) twice, P5, K1, P 11, K6.

Row 23: K7, P 13, K1, P9, K7.

Row 25: K7, P 14, K1, P7, K8.

Row 27: K7, P 23, K7.

Row 29: K7, P 23, K7.

Row 31: K8, P 22, K7.

Row 33: K9, P1, K 10, P 10, K7.

Row 35: K9, P1, K 10, P2, K6, P2, K7.

Row 37: K9, P1, K 10, P2, K6, P2, K7.

Row 39: K9, P1, K 10, P2, K6, P2, K7.

Row 41: K9, P1, K 10, P 10, K7.

Row 43: K9, P1, K 10, P 10, K7.

Row 45: Knit across.

Row 47: Knit across.

Row 49: Knit across.

Rows 51-57: Knit across.

Bind off all sts in **knit**.

Design by Linda Daley.

Tree Washcloth

Shown on page 10.

Finished Size: 7³/₄" (19.5 cm) square

Materials
Medium Weight
  100% Cotton Yarn
[2.5 ounces, 120 yards
(71 grams, 109 meters) per ball]:
  Green - One ball
  Red - small amount
Straight knitting needles, size 7
  (4.5 mm) **or** size needed for gauge
Yarn needle

Gauge
In Stockinette Stitch,
(knit one row, purl one row)
19 sts = 4" (10 cm)

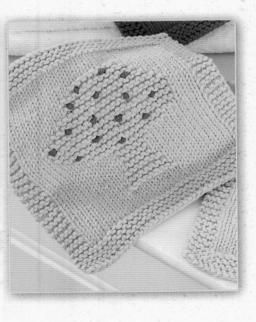

Washcloth
With Green, cast on 37 sts.

Rows 1-7: Knit across.

Row 8: K4, P 29, K4.

Row 9 (Right side): Knit across.

Row 10 AND ALL WRONG SIDE ROWS THRU Row 50: K4, P 29, K4.

Row 11: Knit across.

Row 13: K 14, P9, K 14.

Row 15: K 15, P7, K 15.

Row 17: K 15, P7, K 15.

Row 19: K 16, P5, K 16.

Row 21: K 16, P5, K 16.

Row 23: K 15, P6, K 16.

Row 25: K 11, P 14, K 12.

Row 27: K9, P 18, K 10.

Row 29: K8, P 20, K9.

Row 31: K8, P 21, K8.

Row 33: K8, P 21, K8.

Row 35: K8, P 21, K8.

Row 37: K9, P 18, K 10.

Row 39: K 10, P 15, P 12.

Row 41: K 11, P 12, K 14.

Row 43: K 12, P 11, K 14.

Row 45: K 13, P8, K 16.

Row 47: Knit across.

Row 49: Knit across.

Rows 51-57: Knit across.

Bind off all sts in **knit**.

With Red, add French knots for apples as follows: Bring needle up at 1. Wrap yarn around the needle the desired number of times and insert needle at 2, holding end of yarn with non-stitching fingers **(Fig. A)**. Tighten knot; then pull needle through, holding yarn until it must be released.

Fig. A

Design by Linda Daley.

Blanket

Shown on page 2.

Finished Size: 35" x 45"
(89 cm x 114.5 cm)

Materials
Medium Weight Yarn
[1.75 ounces, 140 yards
(50 grams, 128 meters) per skein]:
  7 skeins
29" (73.5 cm) Circular knitting
  needle, size 11 (8 mm) **or** size
  needed for gauge

Gauge
In pattern, 14 sts and 20 rows =
  4" (10 cm)
Rows 1-22 (corner triangle) =
  5" x 5" x 6³/₄"
(12.75 cm x 12.75 cm x 17.25 cm)

Note: Blanket is worked diagonally
from lower corner to opposite
top corner.

Body
Cast on one st.

Row 1: Increase (**Figs. 7a & b,
page 39**): 2 sts.

Row 2: Increase, K1: 3 sts.

Rows 3-6: Increase, knit across:
7 sts.

Rows 7-159: K3, YO (**Fig. 6,
page 39**), knit across: 160 sts.

Row 160: K2, K2 tog (**Fig. 12,
page 40**), YO, K2 tog, knit across:
159 sts.

Row 161: K3, YO, knit across:
160 sts.

Repeat Rows 160 and 161 until
increase edge of Body measures
approximately 45" (114.5 cm) from
cast on stitch, ending by working
Row 161: 160 sts.

Decrease Row: K2, K2 tog, YO,
K2 tog, knit across: 159 sts.

Repeat Decrease Row until 7 sts
remain on needle.

Next 5 Rows: K2 tog, knit across:
2 sts.

Last Row: K2 tog; cut yarn and
pull through last st: one st.

Design by John Feddersen, Jr.

14

Booties

Shown on page 3.

Size: 0-3 months {3-6 months}

Size Note: Instructions are written for size 0-3 months with size 3-6 months in braces { }. Instructions will be easier to read if you circle all the numbers pertaining to your child's size. If only one number is given, it applies to both sizes.

Materials
Medium Weight Yarn
[3 ounces, 185 yards
(85 grams, 170 meters) per skein]:
  Brown - 1 skein
  Coral - 1 skein
Straight knitting needles, size 7
  (4.5 mm) **or** size needed
  for gauge
Stitch holder
Markers
1/4" (7 mm) Buttons - 6
Sewing needle and thread
Tapestry needle

Gauge
In Garter Stitch, 10 sts and
20 rows = 2" (5 cm)

Right Bootie
Sole
With Brown, cast on 38{44} sts.

Row 1 (Right side): Knit across, place marker around any st to mark **right** side (*see Markers, page 38*).

Row 2: K 18{20}, place marker, increase (*Figs. 7a & b, page 39*), K 0{2} (*see Zeros, page 36*), increase, place marker, knit across: 40{46} sts.

Rows 3-6: Knit across to first marker, increase, knit across to within one st of next marker, increase, knit across: 48{54} sts.

Row 7: Knit across to first marker, remove marker, increase, knit across to within one st of next marker, increase, remove marker, knit across: 50{56} sts.

Instep
Row 1: K 14{16}, place marker, [slip 1 as if to **knit**, K1, PSSO (*Fig. 18, page 41*)], K 18{20}, K2 tog (*Fig. 12, page 40*), place marker, knit across; cut Brown: 48{54} sts.

Rows 2-5: With Coral, knit across to first marker, slip 1 as if to **knit**, K1, PSSO, knit across to within 2 sts of next marker, K2 tog, knit across: 40{46} sts.

Row 6: Knit across to first marker, remove marker, slip 1 as if to **knit**, K1, PSSO, knit across to within 2 sts of next marker, K2 tog, remove marker, knit across: 38{44} sts.

Row 7: K 14{16}, slip 1 as if to **knit**, K1, PSSO, K1, slip 16{18} sts just worked onto st holder, bind off next 4{6} sts, K2 tog, knit across: 16{18} sts.

First Side
Row 1: Knit across to last 4 sts, K2 tog twice: 14{16} sts.

Row 2: (Slip 1 as if to **knit**, K1, PSSO) twice, knit across: 12{14} sts.

Row 3: Knit across.

Row 4: Add on 12{14} sts (*Figs. 3a & b, page 38*), knit across: 24{28} sts.

Row 5 (Buttonhole row): Knit across to last 2 sts, YO (*Fig. 6, page 39*), K2 tog.

Row 6: Bind off 12{14} sts **loosely** in **knit**, knit across: 12{14} sts.

Instructions continued on page 16.

Rows 7-13: Repeat Rows 3-6 once, then repeat Rows 3-5 once **more**.

Bind off all sts **loosely** in **knit**.

Second Side
Row 1: Slip 16{18} sts from st holder onto empty needle; (slip 1 as if to **knit**, K1, PSSO) twice, knit across: 14{16} sts.

Row 2: Knit across to last 4 sts, K2 tog twice: 12{14} sts.

Rows 3-13: Knit across.

Bind off all sts **loosely** in **knit**.

With right sides together, sew Sole and back in one continuous seam.

Sew buttons to side opposite straps.

Left Bootie
Marking Row 2 of Sole as **right** side, work same as Right Bootie through Row 7 of Sole; at end of Row 7, cut Brown.

Instep
Row 1: With Coral, K 14{16}, place marker, slip 1 as if to **knit**, K1, PSSO, K 18{20}, K2 tog, place marker, knit across: 48{54} sts.

Beginning with Row 2 of Instep, complete same as Right Bootie.

Design by Sandra J. Patterson.

Cardigan

🔳🔳🔳🔲🔲 INTERMEDIATE

Shown on page 4.

Size
{3 months-6 months}
{12 months-18 months-24 months}

Finished Chest Measurement
{21-22}{23-24-25¹/₂}"/
{53.5-56}{58.5-61-65} cm

Size Note: Instructions are written with sizes 3 months and 6 months in the first set of braces { } and with sizes 12 months, 18 months, and 24 months in the second set of braces. Instructions will be easier to read if you circle all the numbers pertaining to your child's size. If only one number is given, it applies to all sizes.

Materials
Light Weight Yarn
[4.25 ounces, 333 yards
(120 grams, 304 meters)
per skein]:
  (MC) Variegated - 2 skeins
[5 ounces, 395 yards
(140 grams, 361 meters)
per skein]:
  (CC) White - 1 skein
Straight knitting needles, sizes
  5 (3.75 mm) **and** 6 (4 mm) **or**
  sizes needed for gauge
24" (61 cm) Circular needle, size 5
  (3.75 mm)
Cable needle
Markers
Stitch holder
¹/₂" (12 mm) Buttons - 4
Tapestry needle
Sewing needle and matching thread

Gauge
With larger size needles, in pattern,
  22 sts and 30 rows = 4" (10 cm)

Stitch Guide
Front Cable (uses next 3 sts)
Slip next st onto cable needle and hold in **front** of work, knit next 2 sts from left needle, K1 from cable needle.
Back Cable (uses next 3 sts)
Slip next 2 sts onto cable needle and hold in **back** of work, knit next st from left needle, K2 from cable needle.

Back
Ribbing

For Sizes 3, 6, & 12 Months Only
With MC and using smaller size straight needles, cast on {59-61}{65} sts.

Row 1: P1, (K1, P1) across.

Row 2 (Right side): Knit across.

Row 3: P1, (K1, P1) across; drop MC.

Row 4: With CC, knit across.

Row 5: P1, (K1, P1) across; cut CC.

Row 6: With MC, knit across.

Rows 7 and 8: Repeat Rows 1 and 2.

For Sizes 18 & 24 Months Only
With MC and using smaller size straight needles, cast on {67-71} sts.

Row 1: P1, (K1, P1) across.

Row 2 (Right side): Knit across.

Row 3: P1, (K1, P1) across.

Rows 4 and 5: Repeat Rows 2 and 3; at end of Row 5, drop MC.

Row 6: With CC, knit across.

Row 7: P1, (K1, P1) across; cut CC.

Row 8: With MC, knit across.

Rows 9-12: Repeat Rows 1 and 2 twice.

For All Sizes
Row {9-9}{9-13-13}: P1, (K1, P1) across increasing one st **(Figs. 7a & b, page 39):** {60-62}{66-68-72} sts.

Body
Change to larger size needles.

Row 1: K{2-3}{5-6-2}, P2, (K4, P2) {9-9}{9-9-11} times, K{2-3}{5-6-2}.

Row 2: Purl across.

Row 3: K{5-6}{2-3-5}, P2, (K4, P2) {8-8}{10-10-10} times, K{5-6}{2-3-5}.

Row 4: Purl across.

Repeat Rows 1-4 until Back measures approximately {11-11½}{12½-13-14}"/{28-29}{32-33-35.5} cm from cast on edge, ending by working a **wrong** side row.

Last Row: Bind off {20-21}{22-23-25} sts, knit next {19-19}{21-21-21} sts, slip {20-20}{22-22-22} sts just worked onto st holder; bind off remaining sts.

Left Front
Ribbing

For Sizes 3, 6, & 12 Months Only
With MC and using smaller size straight needles, cast on {25-27}{29} sts.

Row 1: P1, (K1, P1) across.

Row 2 (Right side): Knit across.

Row 3: P1, (K1, P1) across; drop MC.

Row 4: With CC, knit across.

Row 5: P1, (K1, P1) across; cut CC.

Row 6: With MC, knit across.

Rows 7 and 8: Repeat Rows 1 and 2.

Instructions continued on page 18.

Back

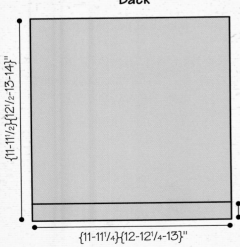

{11-11½}{12½-13-14}"

{11-11¼}{12-12¼-13}"

{1-1}{1-1½-1½}"

Left Front

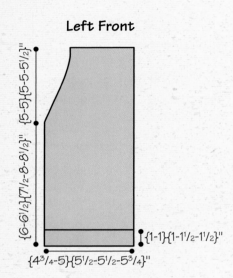

{5-5}{5-5-5½}"

{6-6½}{7½-8-8½}"

{1-1}{1-1½-1½}"

{4¾-5}{5½-5½-5¾}"

For Sizes 18 & 24 Months Only
With MC and using smaller size straight needles, cast on {29-31} sts.

Row 1: P1, (K1, P1) across.

Row 2 (Right side): Knit across.

Row 3: P1, (K1, P1) across.

Rows 4 and 5: Repeat Rows 2 and 3; at end of Row 5, drop MC.

Row 6: With CC, knit across.

Row 7: P1, (K1, P1) across; cut CC.

Row 8: With MC, knit across.

Rows 9-12: Repeat Rows 1 and 2 twice.

For All Sizes
Row {9-9}{9-13-13}: P1, (K1, P1) across increasing one st: {26-28} {30-30-32} sts.

Body
Change to larger size needles.

Row 1: K{1-3}{5-5-1}, P2, (K4, P2) {2-2}{2-2-3} times, place marker (*see Markers, page 38*), K9, P1, K1.

Row 2 AND ALL WRONG SIDE ROWS: P2, K1, purl across.

Row 3: K{4-6}{2-2-4}, P2, (K4, P2) {1-1}{2-2-2} time(s), K 12, P1, K1.

Row 5: K{1-3}{5-5-1}, P2, (K4, P2) {2-2}{2-2-3} times, K1, work Front Cable, work Back Cable, K2, P1, K1.

Row 7: K{4-6}{2-2-4}, (P2, K4) {2-2}{3-3-3} times, work Front Cable, work Back Cable, K2, P1, K1.

Row 9: K{1-3}{5-5-1}, P2, (K4, P2) {2-2}{2-2-3} times, K1, work Front Cable, work Back Cable, K2, P1, K1.

Row 11: K{4-6}{2-2-4}, P2, (K4, P2) {1-1}{2-2-2} time(s), K 12, P1, K1.

Row 13: K{1-3}{5-5-1}, P2, (K4, P2) {2-2}{2-2-3} times, K9, P1, K1.

Row 15: K{4-6}{2-2-4}, (P2, K4) {2-2}{3-3-3} times, work Front Cable, work Back Cable, K2, P1, K1.

Row 17: K{1-3}{5-5-1}, P2, (K4, P2) {2-2}{2-2-3} times, K1, work Front Cable, work Back Cable, K2, P1, K1.

Row 19: K{4-6}{2-2-4}, (P2, K4) {2-2}{3-3-3} times, work Front Cable, work Back Cable, K2, P1, K1.

Row 21: K{1-3}{5-5-1}, P2, (K4, P2) {2-2}{2-2-3} times, K9, P1, K1.

Repeat Rows 2-21 until Left Front measures approximately {6-6½}{7½-8-8½}"/{15-16.5} {19-20.5-21.5} cm from cast on edge, ending by working a **wrong** side row.

Neck Shaping

Note: Maintain established pattern throughout.

Row 1 (Decrease row): Work across to within 3 sts of marker, K2 tog **(Fig. 12, page 40)**, K1, work across, place marker around last st to mark beginning of Neck Shaping: {25-27}{29-29-31} sts.

Rows 2-4: Work across.

Continue to decrease in same manner, every fourth row, {1-4} {7-4-1} time(s); then decrease every sixth row, {4-2}{0-2-5} times **(see Zeros, page 36)**: {20-21}{22-23-25} sts.

Work even until Left Front measures same as Back, ending by working a **wrong** side row.

Bind off remaining sts in **knit**.

Right Front
Ribbing
For Sizes 3, 6, & 12 Months Only
With MC and using smaller size straight needles, cast on {25-27} {29} sts.

Row 1: P1, (K1, P1) across.

Row 2 (Right side): Knit across.

Row 3: P1, (K1, P1) across; drop MC.

Row 4: With CC, knit across.

Row 5: P1, (K1, P1) across; cut CC.

Row 6: With MC, knit across.

Rows 7 and 8: Repeat Rows 1 and 2.

For Sizes 18 & 24 Months Only
With MC and using smaller size straight needles, cast on {29-31} sts.

Row 1: P1, (K1, P1) across.

Row 2 (Right side): Knit across.

Row 3: P1, (K1, P1) across.

Rows 4 and 5: Repeat Rows 2 and 3; end of Row 5, drop MC.

Row 6: With CC, knit across.

Row 7: P1, (K1, P1) across; cut CC.

Row 8: With MC, knit across.

Rows 9-12: Repeat Rows 1 and 2 twice.

For All Sizes
Row {9-9}{9-13-13}: P1, (K1, P1) across increasing one st: {26-28} {30-30-32} sts.

Body
Change to larger size needles.

Row 1: K1, P1, K9, place marker, P2, (K4, P2) {2-2}{2-2-3} times, K{1-3} {5-5-1}.

Row 2 AND ALL WRONG SIDE ROWS: Purl across to last 3 sts, K1, P2.

Row 3: K1, P1, K 12, P2, (K4, P2) {1-1}{2-2-2} time(s), K{4-6}{2-2-4}.

Row 5: K1, P1, K2, work Front Cable, work Back Cable, K1, P2, (K4, P2) {2-2}{2-2-3} times, K{1-3}{5-5-1}.

Row 7: K1, P1, K2, work Front Cable, work Back Cable, (K4, P2) {2-2} {3-3-3} times, K{4-6}{2-2-4}.

Row 9: K1, P1, K2, work Front Cable, work Back Cable, K1, P2, (K4, P2) {2-2}{2-2-3} times, K{1-3}{5-5-1}.

Row 11: K1, P1, K 12, P2, (K4, P2) {1-1}{2-2-2} time(s), K{4-6}{2-2-4}.

Row 13: K1, P1, K9, P2, (K4, P2) {2-2}{2-2-3} times, K{1-3}{5-5-1}.

Row 15: K1, P1, K2, work Front Cable, work Back Cable, (K4, P2) {2-2}{3-3-3} times, K{4-6}{2-2-4}.

Instructions continued on page 20.

Row 17: K1, P1, K2, work Front Cable, work Back Cable, K1, P2, (K4, P2) {2-2}{2-2-3} times, K{1-3}{5-5-1}.

Row 19: K1, P1, K2, work Front Cable, work Back Cable, (K4, P2) {2-2}{3-3-3} times, K{4-6}{2-2-4}.

Row 21: K1, P1, K9, P2, (K4, P2) {2-2}{2-2-3} times, K{1-3}{5-5-1}.

Repeat Rows 2-21 until Right Front measures same as Left Front to Neck Shaping, ending by working a **wrong** side row.

Neck Shaping

Note: Maintain established pattern throughout.

Row 1 (Decrease row): Work across to marker, K1, SSK **(Figs. 16a-c, page 40)**, work across, place marker around first st to mark beginning of Neck Shaping: {25-27} {29-29-31} sts.

Rows 2-4: Work across.

Continue to decrease in same manner, every fourth row, {1-4} {7-4-1} time(s); then decrease every sixth row, {4-2}{0-2-5} times: {20-21}{22-23-25} sts.

Work even until Right Front measures same as Back, ending by working a **wrong** side row.

Bind off remaining sts in **knit**.

Sleeve (Make 2)
Ribbing

For Sizes 3, 6, & 12 Months Only
With MC and using smaller size straight needles, cast on {35-35} {37} sts.

Row 1: P1, (K1, P1) across.

Row 2 (Right side): Knit across.

Row 3: P1, (K1, P1) across; drop MC.

Row 4: With CC, knit across.

Row 5: P1, (K1, P1) across; cut CC.

Row 6: With MC, knit across.

Rows 7 and 8: Repeat Rows 1 and 2.

For Sizes 18 & 24 Months Only
With MC and using smaller size straight needles, cast on {39-39} sts.

Row 1: P1, (K1, P1) across.

Sleeve

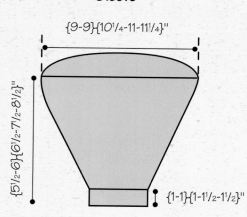

{9-9}{10¼-11-11¼}"

{5½-6}{6½-7½-8½}"

{1-1}{1-1½-1½}"

Row 2 (Right side): Knit across.

Row 3: P1, (K1, P1) across.

Rows 4 and 5: Repeat Rows 2 and 3; at end of Row 5, drop MC.

Row 6: With CC, knit across.

Row 7: P1, (K1, P1) across; cut CC.

Row 8: With MC, knit across.

Rows 9-12: Repeat Rows 1 and 2 twice.

For All Sizes
Row {9-9}{9-13-13}: P1, (K1, P1) across increasing one st: {36-36} {38-40-40} sts.

Body
Change to larger size needles.

Row 1: K{2-2}{3-4-4}, P2, (K4, P2) 5 times, K{2-2}{3-4-4}.

Row 2: Purl across.

Row 3: K1, work Right Invisible Increase **(Fig. 8, page 39)**, K{4-4} {5-0-0}, P2, (K4, P2) {4-4}{4-6-6} times, K{4-4}{5-0-0}, work Left Invisible Increase **(Figs. 9a & b, page 39)**, K1: {38-38}{40-42-42} sts.

Row 4: Purl across.

Row 5 (Increase row): K1, work Right Invisible Increase, K{2-2}{3-4-4}, P2, (K4, P2) 5 times, K{2-2}{3-4-4}, work Left Invisible Increase, K1: {40-40}{42-44-44} sts.

Row 6: Purl across.

Row 7: K{1-1}{2-3-3}, P2, (K4, P2) 6 times, K{1-1}{2-3-3}.

Row 8: Purl across.

Beginning with next row and working new sts in established pattern, increase one st in same manner at **each** edge, every fourth row, {5-5}{7-8-9} times: {50-50}{56-60-62} sts.

Work even until Sleeve measures approximately {5¹⁄₂-6}{6¹⁄₂-7¹⁄₂-8¹⁄₂}"/{14-15}{16.5-19-21.5} cm from cast on edge, ending by working a **wrong** side row.

Sleeve Shaping
Rows 1-8: Bind off {5-5}{6-7-7} sts at the beginning of the row, work across: {10-10}{8-4-6} sts.

Bind off remaining sts in **knit**.

Finishing
Sew shoulder seams.

Band
With **right** side facing, using MC and circular needle, pick up {36-38}{44-48-52} sts evenly spaced across Right Front to marker **(Fig. 20b, page 41)**, do **not** remove marker, pick up {26-32}{32-32-36} sts along Right Front Neck edge, knit {20-20}{22-22-22} sts from Back st holder, pick up {25-31}{31-31-35} sts across Left Front Neck edge to marker, do **not** remove marker, pick up {36-38}{44-48-52} sts evenly spaced across Left Front: {143-159}{173-181-197} sts.

Mark placement of buttonholes on Left Front, placing first marker ¹⁄₂" (12 mm) from cast on edge and second marker ¹⁄₂" (12 mm) down from Neck Shaping marker; evenly space markers for remaining 2 buttons.

Row 1: P1, (K1, P1) across.

Row 2: Knit across.

Row 3: P1, (K1, P1) across; drop MC.

Row 4 (Buttonhole row): With CC, knit across to first marker, [K2 tog, YO **(Fig. 6, page 39)**, **(buttonhole made)]**, (knit across to next marker, K2 tog, YO) 3 times, knit across.

Row 5: P1, (K1, P1) across; cut CC.

Row 6: With MC, knit across.

Row 7: P1, (K1, P1) across.

Bind off all sts in **knit**.

Sew Sleeves to Cardigan, matching center of last row on Sleeve Shaping to shoulder seam and beginning {4¹⁄₂-4¹⁄₂}{5-5¹⁄₂-5¹⁄₂}"/{11.5-11.5}{12.5-14-14} cm down from seam.

Weave underarm and side in one continuous seam **(Fig. 21, page 42)**.

Sew buttons to Band opposite buttonholes.

Design by Lois J. Long.

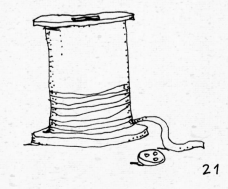

21

Striped Hat

Shown on page 5.

Size: 9-12 months
Finished Measurement: 16³/₄"
(42.5 cm)

Materials
Medium Weight Yarn
[3 ounces, 185 yards
(85 grams, 170 meters) per skein]:
   Yellow - 1 skein
   Purple - 1 skein
   Rose - 1 skein
   Dk Purple - 1 skein
   Green - small amount
Set of 5 double pointed knitting
   needles, size 6 (4 mm) **or** size
   needed for gauge
Straight knitting needles, size 6
   (4 mm) **or** size needed for gauge
Split-ring marker
Yarn needle

Gauge
In Stockinette Stitch,
22 sts and 28 rnds = 4" (10 cm)

Body
With Yellow, cast on 92 sts.

Divide sts onto 4 needles **(see
Double Pointed Needles, page 38)**,
placing 23 sts on each needle.

Place a split-ring marker around
the first stitch to indicate the
beginning of the round **(see
Markers, page 38)**.

Knit 18 rnds.

With Purple, knit 5 rnds.

With Rose, knit 7 rnds.

With Dk Purple, knit 3 rnds.

Crown Shaping
Rnd 1: K9, K2 tog **(Fig. 12,
page 40)**, (K7, K2 tog) around:
82 sts.

Rnd 2: Knit around.

Rnd 3: K8, K2 tog, (K6, K2 tog)
around: 72 sts.

Rnd 4: Knit around.

Rnd 5: (K4, K2 tog) around:
60 sts.

Rnd 6: Knit around.

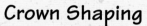

Rnd 7: (K3, K2 tog) around:
48 sts.

Rnd 8: Knit around.

Rnd 9: (K2, K2 tog) around:
36 sts.

Rnd 10: Knit around.

Rnd 11: (K1, K2 tog) around: 24 sts.

Rnd 12: Knit around.

Rnd 13: K2 tog around: 12 sts.

Rnd 14: Knit around.

Rnd 15: K2 tog around; cut yarn
leaving a long end for sewing: 6 sts.

Thread yarn needle with long end
and weave through remaining sts
on needles; gather **tightly** to close
and secure end.

Leaf

With straight needles and Green, cast on 3 sts.

Row 1: K1, ★ YO *(Fig. 6, page 39)*, K1; repeat from ★ once **more**: 5 sts.

Row 2: Purl across.

Row 3: K2, YO, K1, YO, K2: 7 sts.

Row 4: Purl across.

Row 5: K3, YO, K1, YO, K3: 9 sts.

Row 6: Purl across.

Row 7: Knit across.

Rows 8-10: Repeat Rows 6 and 7 once, then repeat Row 6 once **more**.

Row 11: K3, [slip 2 sts tog as if to **knit**, K1, P2SSO *(Figs. 19a & b, page 41)*], K3: 7 sts.

Row 12: Purl across.

Row 13: K2, slip 2 sts tog as if to **knit**, K1, P2SSO, K2: 5 sts.

Row 14: Purl across.

Row 15: K1, slip 2 sts tog as if to **knit**, K1, P2SSO, K1: 3 sts.

Row 16: Purl across.

Row 17: Slip 2 sts tog as if to **knit**, K1, P2SSO; cut yarn leaving a long end for sewing; pull yarn through last st.

Flower

With straight needles and Purple, cast on 62 sts.

Row 1: Purl across.

Row 2 (Right side): K3, slip last st back onto left needle **(base st)**, pass the next 8 sts on left needle over the base st, † give the working yarn a slight tug to tighten the petal, YO twice **(Fig. A)**, knit the base st again and next 3 sts, slip the last st back onto left needle **(base st)** †, pass the next 12 sts on left needle over the base st, repeat from † to † once, pass the next 8 sts on left needle over the base st, repeat from † to † once, pass the next 10 sts on left needle over the base st, repeat from † to † once, pass the next 7 sts on left needle over the base st, give the working yarn a slight tug to tighten the petal, YO twice, knit the base st again and last 2 sts; cut Purple: 27 sts.

Fig. A

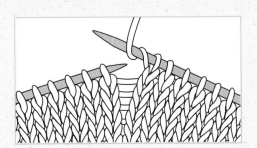

Row 3: ★ With Yellow, P1, P2 tog *(Fig. 14, page 40)*, purl into the front of the first YO, purl into the back of the second YO *(Fig. 4b, page 38)*; repeat from ★ across to last 2 sts, P2: 22 sts.

Row 4: P2 tog across: 11 sts.

Cut yarn leaving a long end for sewing. Thread yarn needle with end and weave through remaining sts, gather **tightly** to close and secure end; do **not** cut yarn. With same end, sew end of rows on first and last petals together and secure end; do **not** cut yarn.

Using photo as a guide for placement and long ends, sew the Leaf and Flower to Hat.

Design by Lois J. Long.

Eyelet Cap

Shown on page 5.

Size: 6-9 months
Finished Size: 16¹/₂" (42 cm)

Materials

Light Weight Yarn
[5 ounces, 459 yards
(141 grams, 420 meters)
per skein]: 1 skein
Set of 5 double pointed knitting
    needles, size 6 (4 mm) **or** size
    needed for gauge
Split-ring marker
Tapestry needle

Gauge

In Stockinette Stitch,
24 sts and 30 rnds = 4" (10 cm)

Body

Cast on 100 sts.

Divide sts onto 4 needles **(see Double Pointed Needles, page 38)**, placing 25 sts on each needle.

Place a split-ring marker around the first stitch to indicate the beginning of the round **(see Markers, page 38)**.

Rnd 1: Purl around.

Rnds 2-5: Knit around.

Rnd 6: K3, K2 tog **(Fig. 12, page 40)**, YO **(Fig. 6, page 39)**, K1, YO, SSK **(Figs. 16a-c, page 40)**, ★ K5, K2 tog, YO, K1, YO, SSK; repeat from ★ around to last 2 sts, K2.

Rnd 7: K5, slip 1 as it to **knit**, (K9, slip 1 as if to **knit**) around to last 4 sts, K4.

Rnds 8 and 9: Repeat Rnds 6 and 7.

Rnds 10-15: Knit around.

Rnd 16: (K1, YO, SSK K5, K2 tog, YO) around.

Rnd 17: (Slip 1 as if to **knit**, K9) around.

Rnds 18 and 19: Repeat Rnds 16 and 17.

Rnds 20-25: Knit around.

Rnds 26-29: Repeat Rnds 6 and 7 twice.

Knit around until Body measures approximately 4³/4" (12 cm) from cast on edge.

Crown Shaping

Rnd 1: (K 23, K2 tog) around: 96 sts.

Rnd 2: Knit around.

Rnd 3: (K6, K2 tog) around: 84 sts.

Rnd 4: Knit around.

Rnd 5: (K5, K2 tog) around: 72 sts.

Rnd 6: Knit around.

Rnd 7: (K4, K2 tog) around: 60 sts.

Rnd 8: Knit around.

Rnd 9: (K3, K2 tog) around: 48 sts.

Rnd 10: Knit around.

Rnd 11: (K2, K2 tog) around: 36 sts.

Rnd 12: Knit around.

Rnd 13: (K1, K2 tog) around: 24 sts.

Rnd 14: Knit around.

Rnd 15: K2 tog around: 12 sts.

Rnd 16: Knit around.

Rnd 17: K2 tog around; cut yarn leaving a long end for sewing: 6 sts.

Thread tapestry needle with long end. Weave through remaining sts on needles; gather **tightly** and secure end.

Ruffle

With **right** side facing, pick up 100 sts around cast on edge **(Fig. 20a, page 41)**, placing 25 stitches on each needle.

Place a split-ring marker around the first stitch to indicate the beginning of the round.

Rnd 1: ★ K1, increase **(Figs. 7a & b, page 39)**; repeat from ★ around: 150 sts.

Rnd 2: (K2 tog, YO) around.

Rnd 3: Knit around.

Rnd 4: (YO, K2 tog) around.

Rnds 5-7: Knit around.

Bind off all sts in **purl**.

Design by Lois J. Long.

Blanket with Pig Hood

■■□□ EASY

Shown on page 7.

Finished Size: 35" x 45"
(89 cm x 114.5 cm)

Materials
Medium Weight Yarn
[3.5 ounces, 171 yards
(100 grams, 156 meters)
per skein]:
   Pink - 6 skeins
   Rose - 1 skein
29" (73.5 cm) Circular knitting
   needle, size 11 (8 mm) **or** size
   needed for gauge
Navy embroidery floss
Yarn needle

Gauge
In pattern, 14 sts and 20 rows =
4" (10 cm)
Rows 1-22 (corner triangle) =
5" x 5" x 6³/₄"
(12.75 cm x 12.75 cm x 17.25 cm)

Blanket
With Pink, work same as Blanket,
page 14.

Hood
With Pink, work same as Blanket,
page 14, through Row 39: 40 sts.

Decrease Row: K2, K2 tog, YO,
K2 tog, knit across: 39 sts.

Repeat Decrease Row until
7 sts remain.

Next Row (Right side): K2 tog,
work Loop St in next 4 sts **(Fig. 5,
page 38)**, K1: 6 sts.

Next Row: K2 tog, knit across:
5 sts.

Next Row: K2 tog, work Loop St in
next 2 sts, K1: 4 sts.

Next Row: K2 tog, K2: 3 sts.

Last Row: K3 tog **(Fig. 13,
page 40)**; cut yarn and pull
through last st.

Nose
With Rose, cast on 7 sts.

Row 1: Increase, K5, increase: 9 sts.

Row 2: Increase, K7, increase:
11 sts.

Rows 3 and 4: Knit across.

Rows 5 and 6: K2 tog, knit across
to last 2 sts, K2 tog: 7 sts.

Bind off remaining sts in **knit**,
leaving a long end for sewing.

Ear (Make 2)
With Rose, cast on one st.

Row 1: Increase: 2 sts.

Rows 2-11: Increase, knit across:
12 sts.

Rows 12-14: Knit across.

Rows 15 and 16: K2 tog, knit
across: 10 sts.

Blanket with Chick Hood

Rows 17-19: Knit across.

Rows 20 and 21: Increase, knit across: 12 sts.

Rows 22-24: Knit across.

Rows 25-34: K2 tog, knit across: 2 sts.

Row 35: K2 tog; cut yarn and pull through last st: one st.

Fold Ear along Row 18 with cast on st and last st together; sew edges together.

Fold Hood in half with **right** side facing and cast on st and last st together. Using photo as a guide for placement, sew Nose and Ears to **right** side of Hood. Pin Hood to corner of Blanket. Using Pink and working through all 3 layers, sew Hood to Blanket.

Using photo as a guide and floss, add buttonhole stitch eyes as follows: Come up at 1, go down at 2, and come up at 3, keeping floss below point of needle **(Fig. A)**.

Fig. A

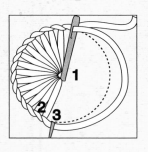

■■□□□ **EASY**

Shown on page 6.

Finished Size: 35" x 45" (89 cm x 114.5 cm)

Materials
Medium Weight Yarn ⟮**MEDIUM 4**⟯
[3.5 ounces, 171 yards (100 grams, 156 meters) per skein]:
   Yellow - 6 skeins
   Bright Yellow - 1 skein
   Rose - small amount
29" (73.5 cm) Circular knitting
   needle, size 11 (8 mm) **or** size
   needed for gauge
Navy embroidery floss
Yarn needle

Gauge
In pattern, 14 sts and 20 rows = 4" (10 cm)
Rows 1-22 (corner triangle) = 5" x 5" x 6³/₄"
(12.75 cm x 12.75 cm x 17.25 cm)

Blanket
With Yellow, work same as Blanket, page 14.

Hood
With Yellow, work same as Pig Hood, page 26.

Beak
With Bright Yellow, cast on one st.

Row 1: Increase: 2 sts.

Instructions continued on page 28.

Hood design by Sarah J. Green.

Rows 2-11: Increase, knit across: 12 sts.

Rows 12-14: Knit across.

Rows 15-24: K2 tog, knit across: 2 sts.

Row 25: K2 tog; cut yarn and pull through last st.

Tongue

With Rose, cast on 5 sts.

Bind off all sts in **knit**, leaving a long end for sewing.

Fold Hood in half with **right** side facing and cast on st and last st together. Using photo as a guide for placement, sew Beak to **right** side of Hood. Sew Tongue to center of Beak. Pin Hood to corner of Blanket. Using Yellow and working through all 3 layers, sew Hood to Blanket.

Using photo as a guide and floss, add buttonhole stitch eyes **(Fig. A, page 27)**.

Hood design by Sarah J. Green.

Piggie

■■■■◻ **INTERMEDIATE**

Shown on page 8.

Finished Size: 13½" (34.5 cm) tall

Materials

Medium Weight Yarn
[3.5 ounces, 153 yards
(100 grams, 139 meters)
per skein]:
   Pink - 1 skein
   Rose - 1 skein
   Black - small amount
Straight knitting needles, size 8
   (5 mm) **or** size needed for gauge
Stitch holder
Yarn needle
Polyester fiberfill
⅝" (16 mm) wide Ribbon - 22"
(56 cm) long (optional)

Gauge
In Stockinette Stitch
(knit one row, purl one row),
13 sts and 18 rows = 3" (7.5 cm)

Front
Arms
Note: Both Arms are worked at the same time, using separate yarn for each.

With Rose, cast on 5 sts; with second Rose, cast on 5 sts.

Rows 1-3: Knit across; with second yarn, knit across.

Cut each Rose.

Row 4: With Pink, purl across; with second Pink, purl across.

Row 5 (Right side): Knit across; with second yarn, knit across.

Rows 6-12: Repeat Rows 4 and 5, 3 times, then repeat Row 4 once **more**.

Cut yarn and slip Arms onto st holder.

Legs
Work same as Arms through Row 12; do **not** cut yarn.

Row 13: K1, M1 **(Figs. 10a & b, page 39)**, K4; with second yarn, K4, M1, K1: 6 sts on **each** Leg.

Row 14: Purl across, cut yarn; with second yarn, purl across; do **not** cut yarn.

Row 15 (Joining row): K1, M1, K5, **turn;** add on 5 sts **(Figs. 3a & b, page 38), turn;** working across second Leg, K5, M1, K1: 19 sts.

Body
Row 1: Purl across.

Row 2 (Increase row): K1, M1, knit across to last st, M1, K1: 21 sts.

Rows 3-14: Repeat Rows 1 and 2, 6 times: 33 sts.

Rows 15-19: Work even.

Row 20: K1, SSK **(Figs. 16a-c, page 40),** knit across to last 3 sts, K2 tog **(Fig. 12, page 40),** K1: 31 sts.

Rows 21-25: Work even.

Row 26 (Decrease row): K1, SSK, knit across to last 3 sts, K2 tog, K1: 29 sts.

Row 27: Purl across.

Rows 28-30: Repeat Rows 26 and 27 once, then repeat Row 26 once **more:** 25 sts.

Row 31 (Arm joining): Slip one Arm onto empty needle with **purl** side facing, with same needle, purl across Body sts; slip second Arm onto empty needle with **purl** side facing, purl across: 35 sts.

Row 32 (Decrease row): K5, SSK, knit across to last 7 sts, K2 tog, K5: 33 sts.

Row 33: Purl across.

Rows 34 and 35: Repeat Rows 32 and 33: 31 sts.

Row 36: K5, SSK, K3, SSK, K7, K2 tog, K3, K2 tog, K5: 27 sts.

Row 37: Purl across.

Row 38: K5, SSK, K1, SSK, K7, K2 tog, K1, K2 tog, K5: 23 sts.

Row 39: P1, P2 tog 3 times **(Fig. 14, page 40),** P9, SSP 3 times **(Fig. 17, page 41),** P1: 17 sts.

Row 40: K3, SSK, K7, K2 tog, K3: 15 sts.

Row 41: P1, P2 tog 3 times, P1, SSP 3 times, P1: 9 sts.

Head
Row 1: K4, M1, K1, M1, K4: 11 sts.

Row 2: Purl across.

Row 3: K1, (M1, K4, M1, K1) twice: 15 sts.

Row 4 (Increase row): P1, M1P **(Figs. 11a & b, page 40),** purl across to last st, M1P, P1: 17 sts.

Row 5: K1, (M1, K7, M1, K1) twice: 21 sts.

Row 6: Repeat Row 4: 23 sts.

Row 7: K1, M1, knit across to last st, M1, K1: 25 sts.

Row 8: Purl across.

Row 9: K1, M1, K5, M1, K1, M1, K 11, M1, K1, M1, K5, M1, K1: 31 sts.

Row 10: Purl across.

Row 11: Knit across.

Row 12: Purl across.

Row 13: K1, SSK, knit across to last 3 sts, K2 tog, K1: 29 sts.

Row 14: P1, P2 tog, purl across to last 3 sts, SSP, P1: 27 sts.

Row 15: K1, SSK, K6, K2 tog, K5, SSK, K6, K2 tog, K1: 23 sts.

Row 16: Purl across.

Row 17: K4, SSK, K 11, K2 tog, K4: 21 sts.

Rows 18-20: Repeat Rows 10-12.

Instructions continued on page 30.

Inner Ears

Row 1: With Rose K3 *(Fig. 2, page 38)*, (with Pink K3, with Rose K3) 3 times.

Row 2: With Rose P3, (with Pink P3, with Rose P3) 3 times.

Row 3: With Rose K1, † (M1, K1) twice, with Pink [slip 2 sts tog as if to **knit**, K1, P2SSO *(Figs. 19a & b, page 41)*], with Rose K1, (M1, K1) twice †, with Pink bind off next 3 sts, with second Rose and Pink, repeat from † to † once: 11 sts on **each** Ear.

Row 4: With Rose P5, with Pink P1, with Rose P5; with second Rose P5, with second Pink P1, with second Rose P5; cut both Pinks.

Row 5: K4, slip 2 sts tog as if to **knit**, K1, P2SSO, K4; with second yarn, K4, slip 2 sts tog as if to **knit**, K1, P2SSO, K4: 9 sts on **each** Ear.

Row 6: Purl across; with second yarn, purl across.

Row 7: K1, SSK, slip 2 sts tog as if to **knit**, K1, P2SSO, K2 tog, K1; with second yarn, K1, SSK, slip 2 sts tog as if to **knit**, K1, P2SSO, K2 tog, K1: 5 sts on **each** Ear.

Row 8: Purl across; with second yarn, purl across.

Row 9: Knit across; with second yarn, knit across.

Row 10: Purl across; with second yarn, purl across.

Row 11: K1, slip 2 sts tog as if to **knit**, K1, P2SSO, K1; with second yarn, K1, slip 2 sts tog as if to **knit**, K1, P2SSO, K1: 3 sts on **each** Ear.

Row 12: P3; with second yarn, P3.

Row 13: K3 tog *(Fig. 13, page 40)*, cut yarn and pull through st; with second yarn, K3 tog, cut yarn and pull through st.

Back
Tail
With Pink, cast on 8 sts.

Row 1: [K, K1 tbl *(Fig. 4a, page 38)*, K] in each st across: 24 sts.

Bind off all sts **tightly** in **purl**; cut yarn but do **not** pull yarn through last st, slip Tail onto st holder.

Arms, Legs, & Body
Work same as Front through Row 11 of Body: 29 sts.

Row 12 (Tail joining): K1, M1, K 13, slip Tail from st holder onto left hand needle, K2 tog, K 13, M1, K1: 31 sts.

Complete Body same as Front through Row 20 of Head: 21 sts.

Outer Ears

Row 1: K1, M1, K8, M1, K3, M1, K8, M1, K1: 25 sts.

Row 2: Purl across.

Row 3: K1, † (M1, K1) twice, slip 2 sts tog as if to **knit**, K1, P2SSO, K3, (M1, K1) twice †, bind off next 3 sts, with second yarn, repeat from † to † once: 13 sts on **each** Ear.

Row 4: Purl across; with second yarn, purl across.

Row 5: K5, slip 2 sts tog as if to **knit**, K1, P2SSO, K5; with second yarn, K5, slip 2 sts tog as if to **knit**, K1, P2SSO, K5: 11 sts on **each** Ear.

Row 6: Purl across; with second yarn, purl across.

Row 7: K1, SSK, K1, slip 2 sts tog as if to **knit**, K1, P2SSO, K1, K2 tog, K1; with second yarn, K1, SSK, K1, slip 2 sts tog as if to **knit**, K1, P2SSO, K1, K2 tog, K1: 7 sts on **each** Ear.

Row 8: Purl across; with second yarn, purl across.

Row 9: Knit across; with second yarn, knit across.

Row 10: Purl across; with second yarn, purl across.

Row 11: K2, slip 2 sts tog as if to **knit**, K1, P2SSO, K2; with second yarn, K2, slip 2 sts tog as if to **knit**, K1, P2SSO, K2: 5 sts on **each** Ear.

Row 12: Purl across; with second yarn, purl across.

Row 13: K1, K3 tog, K1; with second yarn, K1, K3 tog, K1: 3 sts on **each** Ear.

Row 14: P3 tog **(Fig. 15, page 40)**, cut yarn and pull through st; with second yarn, P3 tog, cut yarn and pull through st.

Nose
With Rose, cast on 4 sts.

Beginning with a **purl** row, work in Stockinette Stitch for 18 rows; bind off all sts in **purl** leaving a long end for sewing.

With **knit** side together, sew cast on and bind off ends together.

Snout
With Rose, cast on 5 sts.

Row 1: Purl across.

Row 2: K1, M1, K3, M1, K1: 7 sts.

Row 3: P1, M1P, P5, M1P, P1: 9 sts.

Row 4: K3, slip 2 sts tog as if to **knit**, K1, P2SSO, K3: 7 sts.

Row 5: P1, (P2 tog, P1) twice: 5 sts.

Bind off all sts in **knit**, leaving a long end for sewing.

Sew Snout to one edge of Nose, centering seam on center st of last row; then sew Nose to Head having seam at bottom.

With Black, duplicate stitch 2 sts at either side of Nose for eyes **(Figs. 22a & b, page 42)**, leaving 7 sts between eyes.

Finishing
With Pink, weave each side seam from Leg to Ear **(Fig. 21, page 42)**, leaving ends of Arms, Legs, top of Head, and bottom edge of Body open. With Pink, sew through the two layers of the Ears across the Head edge to shape and to close off from stuffing. Stuff Head and Body lightly. With Pink, weave inner Leg seams and sew bottom edge of Body closed. With Pink, sew top of Head closed. With Rose, sew ends of Legs and Arms closed.

Tie ribbon in a bow around neck if desired.

Design by Sarah J. Green.

Cow

■■■□ INTERMEDIATE

Shown on page 9.

Finished Size: 14³/₄" (37.5 cm) tall

Materials
Medium Weight Yarn **4**
[3.5 ounces, 153 yards
(100 grams, 139 meters) per skein]:
  Black - 1 skein
  White - 1 skein
  Pink - small amount
Straight knitting needles, size 8
  (5 mm) **or** size needed for gauge
Stitch holder
Yarn needle
Polyester fiberfill
⁵/₈" (16 mm) wide Ribbon - 22"
(56 cm) long (optional)

Gauge
In Stockinette Stitch
(knit one row, purl one row),
13 sts and 18 rows = 3" (7.5 cm)

Back
Arms
Note: Both Arms are worked at
the same time, using separate
yarn for each.

With Black, cast on 5 sts; with
second Black, cast on 5 sts.

Rows 1-3: Knit across; with second
yarn, knit across.

Row 4: Purl across; with second
yarn, purl across.

Row 5 (Right side): Knit across;
with second yarn, knit across.

Rows 6-13: Repeat Rows 4 and 5,
4 times.

Cut yarn and slip Arms onto
st holder.

Legs
Work same as Arms through
Row 12.

Row 13: K1, M1 **(Figs. 10a & b,
page 39)**, K4; with second yarn,
K4, M1, K1: 6 sts on **each** Leg.

Row 14: Purl across, cut yarn; with
second yarn, purl across; do **not**
cut yarn.

Row 15 (Joining row): K1, M1, K5,
turn; add on 5 sts **(Figs. 3a & b,
page 38)**, **turn**; working across
second Leg, K5, M1, K1: 19 sts.

Body
Row 1: Purl across.

Row 2 (Increase row): K1, M1, knit
across to last st, M1, K1: 21 sts.

Row 3: Purl across.

Row 4: Knit across.

Row 5: Purl across.

Rows 6-29: Repeat Rows 2-5,
6 times: 33 sts.

Row 30: K1, SSK **(Figs. 16a-c,
page 40)**, knit across to last
3 sts, K2 tog **(Fig. 12, page 40)**,
K1: 31 sts.

Rows 31-33: Repeat Rows 3-5.

Row 34 (Decrease row): K1, SSK,
knit across to last 3 sts, K2 tog,
K1: 29 sts.

Row 35: Purl across.

Rows 36-38: Repeat Rows 34 and
35 once, then repeat Row 34 once
more: 25 sts.

Row 39 (Arm joining): Slip one
Arm onto empty needle with **purl**
side facing, with same needle, purl
across Body sts; slip second Arm
onto empty needle with **purl** side
facing, purl across: 35 sts.

Row 40 (Decrease row): K5, SSK,
knit across to last 7 sts, K2 tog,
K5: 33 sts.

Row 41: Purl across.

Rows 42 and 43: Repeat Rows 40
and 41: 31 sts.

Row 44: K5, SSK, K3, SSK, K7,
K2 tog, K3, K2 tog, K5: 27 sts.

Row 45: Purl across.

Row 46: K5, SSK, K1, SSK, K7, K2 tog, K1, K2 tog, K5: 23 sts.

Row 47: P1, P2 tog 3 times *(Fig. 14, page 40)*, P9, SSP 3 times *(Fig. 17, page 41)*, P1: 17 sts.

Row 48: K3, SSK, K7, K2 tog, K3: 15 sts.

Row 49: Purl across.

Head

Row 1: K1, M1, knit across to last st, M1, K1: 17 sts.

Row 2: Purl across.

Row 3: Knit across.

Row 4: Purl across.

Row 5: K1, M1, K6, M1, K3, M1, K6, M1, K1: 21 sts.

Row 6: Purl across.

Row 7: K1, M1, knit across to last st, M1, K1: 23 sts.

Rows 8-12: Repeat Rows 2 and 3 twice, then repeat Row 2 once **more**.

Row 13 (Decrease row): K1, SSK, knit across to last 3 sts, K2 tog, K1: 21 sts.

Row 14 (Decrease row): P1, P2 tog, purl across to last 3 sts, SSP, P1: 19 sts.

Rows 15 and 16: Repeat Rows 13 and 14: 15 sts.

Rows 17-20: Repeat Rows 3 and 4 twice.

Ears
Row 1: Bind off 2 sts in **knit**, M1, K3, M1, K1, bind off next st, (M1, K3) twice.

Row 2: Bind off 2 sts in **purl**, P6; with second Black, P7: 7 sts on **each** Ear.

Row 3: K1, M1, K5, M1, K1; with second yarn, K1, M1, K5, M1, K1: 9 sts on **each** Ear.

Row 4: Purl across; with second yarn, purl across.

Row 5: K1, M1, K5, K2 tog, K1; with second yarn, K1, SSK, K5, M1, K1.

Row 6: P1, M1P *(Figs. 11a & b, page 40)*, P5, P2 tog, P1; with second yarn, P1, SSP, P5, M1P, P1.

Row 7: K1, SSK, K3, K2 tog, K1; with second yarn, K1, SSK, K3, K2 tog, K1: 7 sts on **each** Ear.

Row 8: P1, P2 tog, P1, SSP, P1; with second yarn, P1, P2 tog, P1, SSP, P1: 5 sts on **each** Ear.

Row 9: K1, slip 2 tog as if to **knit**, K1, P2SSO, K1; with second yarn, K1, slip 2 tog as if to **knit**, K1, P2SSO, K1: 3 sts on **each** Ear.

Row 10: P3; with second yarn, P3.

Row 11: With Black K1, with Pink K1 *(Fig. 2, page 38)*, with Black K1; with second Black K1, with second Pink K1, with Black K1.

Row 12: With Black P1, with Pink P1, with Black P1; with second Black P1, with Pink P1, with Black P1.

Instructions continued on page 34.

Row 13: With Black K1, with Pink M1, K1, M1, with Black K1; with second Black K1, with Pink M1, K1, M1, with Black K1: 5 sts on **each** Ear.

Row 14: With Black P1, with Pink M1P, P3, M1P, with Black P1; with second Black P1, with Pink M1P, P3, M1P, with Black P1: 7 sts on **each** Ear.

Row 15: With Black K1, with Pink M1, K5, M1, with Black K1; with second Black K1, with Pink, M1, K5, M1, with Black K1: 9 sts on **each** Ear.

Row 16: With Black, P1, with Pink P5, P2 tog, with Black, P1; with second Black P1, with Pink P2 tog, P5, with Black, P1: 8 sts on **each** Ear; cut each Pink.

Row 17: Knit across to last 2 sts, K2 tog; with second yarn, K2 tog, knit across: 7 sts on **each** Ear.

Bind off all sts in **purl**, leaving a long end for sewing.

Front
Arms

Note: Both Arms are worked at the same time, using separate yarn for each.

With Black, cast on 5 sts; with second Black, cast on 5 sts.

Rows 1-3: Knit across; with second yarn, knit across.

Row 4: P1, with White P4; with second White P4, with Black P1.

Row 5: K1, with White K4; with second White K4, with Black K1.

Row 6: P2, with White P3; with second White P3, with Black P2.

Row 7: K2, with White K3; with second White K3, with Black K2.

Row 8: P2, with White P3; with second White P3, with Black P2.

Row 9: K3, with White K2; with second White K2, with Black K3.

Row 10: P4, with White P1; with second White P1, with Black P4; cut both Whites.

Row 11: Knit across.

Row 12: Purl across.

Row 13: Knit across.

Cut yarn and slip Arms onto st holder.

Legs

Rows 1-3: Work same as Arms; at end of Row 3, cut Black.

Row 4: With White, purl across; with second White, purl across.

Row 5: Knit across; with second yarn, knit across.

Rows 6-12: Repeat Rows 4 and 5, 3 times; then repeat Row 4 once **more**.

Row 13: K1, M1, K4; with second yarn, K4, M1, K1: 6 sts on **each** Leg.

Row 14: Purl across, cut yarn; with second yarn, purl across; do **not** cut yarn.

Row 15 (Joining row): K1, M1, K5, **turn**; add on 5 sts; **turn**; working across second Leg, K5, M1, K1: 19 sts.

Body

Rows 1-5: Work same as Back: 21 sts.

Row 6: K1, M1, K1, with Black K3, with White knit across to last st, M1, K1: 23 sts.

Row 7: Purl across to last 8 sts, with Black P5, with White P3.

Row 8: K2, with Black K6, with White knit across.

Row 9: Purl across to last 7 sts, with Black P5, with White P2.

Row 10: K1, M1, K2, with Black K3, with White knit across to last st, M1, K1; cut Black: 25 sts.

Row 11: Purl across.

Row 12: Knit across.

Row 13: P4, with Black P2, with White, purl across.

Row 14: K1, M1, K 16, with Black K4, with White K1, with Black K1, with White, K1, M1, K1: 27 sts.

Row 15: P2, with Black P7, with White purl across.

Row 16: Knit across to last 9 sts, with Black K7, with White K2.

Row 17: P3, with Black P6, with White purl across.

Row 18: K1, M1, K 19, with Black K2, with White K4, M1, K1; cut Black: 29 sts.

Rows 19-49: Work same as Back: 15 sts.

Head
Rows 1-20: Work same as Back: 15 sts.

Row 21: Bind off 2 sts in **knit**, knit across: 13 sts.

Row 22: Bind off 2 sts in **purl**, purl across: 11 sts.

Bind off remaining sts in **knit**.

Nose
With Pink, cast on 3 sts.

Row 1: Knit across.

Rows 2 and 3: Add on 2 sts, knit across: 7 sts.

Row 4: Knit across.

Bind off all sts in **knit**.

Muzzle
With White, cast on 5 sts.

Beginning with a **purl** row, work in Stockinette Stitch for 25 rows.

Bind off all sts in **knit**, leaving a long end for sewing.

With **purl** side together, sew cast on and bind off ends together, then sew Nose to one long edge of Muzzle.

Using photo as a guide for placement, sew Muzzle to Head, stuffing lightly before closing. With Black, use straight stitches for nostrils.

With Black, duplicate stitch 2 sts at either side of Nose for eyes **(Figs. 22a & b, page 42)**, leaving 5 sts between eyes.

Horn (Make 2)
With White, cast on 3 sts.

Beginning with a **purl** row, work in Stockinette Stitch for 5 rows.

Bind off all sts in **knit** leaving a long end for sewing.

Thread needle with long end and weave through end of each row and pull **tightly** to curve Horn, secure end.

Finishing
With Black, weave each side seam from Leg to Ear **(Fig. 21, page 42)**, leaving ends of Arms, Legs, top of Head, and bottom edge of Body open. Fold Ears at Row 8 toward front of Head and sew edges together. Pleat sewn Ears across base and with Black, sew through the two layers of the Ears to shape and to close off from stuffing. Stuff Head and Body lightly. With Black, weave inner Leg seams and sew bottom edge of Body closed. With Black, sew top of Head closed. Tack Ears to top of Head. Sew Horns to Head. With Black, sew ends of Legs and Arms closed.

Tie ribbon in a bow around neck if desired.

Design by Sarah J. Green.

General Instructions

Abbreviations

CC	Contrasting Color
cm	centimeters
K	knit
M1	make one
M1P	make one purl
MC	Main Color
mm	millimeters
P	purl
PSSO	pass slipped stitch over
P2SSO	pass 2 slipped stitches over
Rnd(s)	round(s)
SSK	slip, slip, knit
SSP	slip, slip, purl
st(s)	stitch(es)
tbl	through back loop
tog	together
YO	yarn over

★ — work instructions following ★ as many **more** times as indicated in addition to the first time.

† to † — work all instructions from first † to second † **as many** times as specified.

( ) or [ ] — work enclosed instructions **as many** times as specified by the number immediately following **or** work all enclosed instructions in the stitch or space indicated **or** contains explanatory remarks.

colon (:) — the number(s) given after a colon at the end of a row or round denote(s) the number of stitches you should have on that row or round.

work even — work without increasing or decreasing in the established pattern.

Gauge

Exact gauge is **essential** for proper size. Before beginning your project, make a sample swatch in the yarn and needle specified. After completing the swatch, measure it, counting your stitches and rows carefully. If your swatch is larger or smaller than specified, **make another, changing needle size to get the correct gauge**. Keep trying until you find the size needles that will give you the specified gauge. Once proper gauge is obtained, measure width of garment approximately every 3" (7.5 cm) to be sure gauge remains consistent. If you have more rows per inch than specified, use a larger size needle for the purl rows; if fewer, use a smaller size needle for the purl rows.

Zeros

To consolidate the length of an involved pattern, zeros are sometimes used so that all sizes can be combined. For example, increase every sixth row 5{1-0} time(s) means the first size would increase 5 times, the second size would increase once, and the largest size would do nothing.

Yarn Weight Symbol & Names	LACE 0	SUPER FINE 1	FINE 2	LIGHT 3	MEDIUM 4	BULKY 5	SUPER BULKY 6
Type of Yarns in Category	Fingering, size 10 crochet thread	Sock, Fingering, Baby	Sport, Baby	DK, Light Worsted	Worsted, Afghan, Aran	Chunky, Craft, Rug	Bulky, Roving
Knit Gauge Range* in Stockinette St to 4" (10 cm)	33-40** sts	27-32 sts	23-26 sts	21-24 sts	16-20 sts	12-15 sts	6-11 sts
Advised Needle Size Range	000-1	1 to 3	3 to 5	5 to 7	7 to 9	9 to 11	11 and larger

*GUIDELINES ONLY: The chart above reflects the most commonly used gauges and needle sizes for specific yarn categories.

** Lace weight yarns are usually knitted on larger needles to create lacy openwork patterns. Accordingly, a gauge range is difficult to determine. Always follow the gauge stated in your pattern.

KNIT TERMINOLOGY	
UNITED STATES	INTERNATIONAL
gauge =	tension
bind off =	cast off
yarn over (YO) =	yarn forward (yfwd) or yarn around needle (yrn)

KNITTING NEEDLES															
U.S.	0	1	2	3	4	5	6	7	8	9	10	10½	11	13	15	17
U.K.	13	12	11	10	9	8	7	6	5	4	3	2	1	00	000	---
Metric - mm	2	2.25	2.75	3.25	3.5	3.75	4	4.5	5	5.5	6	6.5	8	9	10	12.75

◼◻◻◻ BEGINNER		Projects for first-time knitters using basic knit and purl stitches. Minimal shaping.
◼◼◻◻ EASY		Projects using basic stitches, repetitive stitch patterns, simple color changes, and simple shaping and finishing.
◼◼◼◻ INTERMEDIATE		Projects with a variety of stitches, such as basic cables and lace, simple intarsia, double-pointed needles and knitting in the round needle techniques, mid-level shaping and finishing.
◼◼◼◼ EXPERIENCED		Projects using advanced techniques and stitches, such as short rows, fair isle, more intricate intarsia, cables, lace patterns, and numerous color changes.

Double Pointed Needles

When working on a project that is too small to use circular needles, double pointed needles are required. Divide the stitches into fourths and slip ¼ of the stitches onto each of the double pointed needles, forming a square and leaving the last needle of the set empty (*Fig. 1*). With the last needle, knit across the first needle. You will now have an empty needle with which to knit the stitches from the next needle. Work the first stitch on each needle firmly to prevent gaps.

Fig. 1

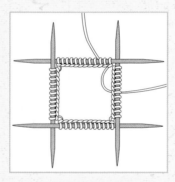

Markers

As a convenience to you, we have used markers to help distinguish the beginning of a round, mark the **right** side of a piece, or the beginning of a pattern. Place markers as instructed. You may use purchased markers or tie a length of contrasting color yarn around the needle. When you reach a marker, slip it from the left needle to the right needle; remove it when no longer needed.

Changing Colors

When changing colors, always pick up the new color yarn from **beneath** the dropped yarn and keep the color which has just been worked to the left (*Fig. 2*). This will prevent holes in your work.

Fig. 2

Adding On Stitches

Insert the right needle into stitch as if to **knit**, yarn over and pull loop through (*Fig. 3a*), insert the left needle into the loop just worked from **front** to **back** and slip the loop onto the left needle (*Fig. 3b*). Repeat for required number of stitches.

Fig. 3a

Fig. 3b

Through Back Loop
(abbreviated tbl)

Insert the right needle into the **back** of the next stitch from **front** to **back** (*Fig. 4a*) for **knit** sts **or** from **back** to **front** (*Fig. 4b*) for **purl** sts, then complete the stitch.

Fig. 4a

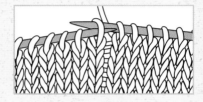

Fig. 4b

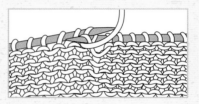

Loop Stitch

K1, do **not** drop st from left needle. With right needle, pull loop just made to measure 1" (2.5 cm) and drop off needle. Knit into back of same st on left needle (*Fig. 5*).

Fig. 5

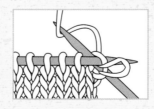

Yarn Over (abbreviated YO)

Bring the yarn forward **between** the needles, then back **over** the top of the right hand needle, so that it is now in position to knit the next stitch **(Fig. 6)**.

Fig. 6

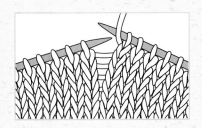

Increase

Knit the next stitch but do **not** slip the old stitch off the left needle **(Fig. 7a)**. Insert the right needle into the **back** loop of the **same** stitch and knit it **(Fig. 7b)**, then slip the old stitch off the left needle.

Fig. 7a

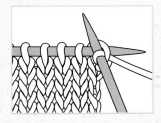

Fig. 7b

Right Invisible Increase

Insert the right needle from the **front** into the side of the stitch **below** the next stitch on the left needle **(Fig. 8)** and knit it.

Fig. 8

Left Invisible Increase

Insert the left needle from the **back** into the side of the stitch 2 rows **below** the stitch on the right needle **(Fig. 9a)**, pull it up and knit into the back loop **(Fig. 9b)**.

Fig. 9a

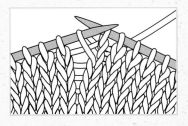

Fig. 9b

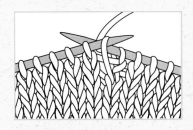

Make One (abbreviated M1)

Insert the **left** needle under the horizontal strand between the stitches from the front **(Fig. 10a)**. Then knit into the **back** of the strand **(Fig. 10b)**.

Fig. 10a

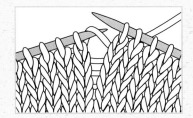

Fig. 10b

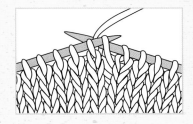

Make One Purl
(abbreviated M1P)

Insert the **left** needle under the horizontal strand between the stitches from the **front** (*Fig. 11a*). Then purl into the **back** of the strand (*Fig. 11b*).

Fig. 11a

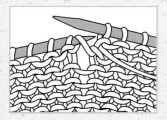

Fig. 11b

Knit 2 Together
(abbreviated K2 tog)

Insert the right needle into the **front** of the first two stitches on the left needle as if to **knit** (*Fig. 12*), then **knit** them together as if they were one stitch.

Fig. 12

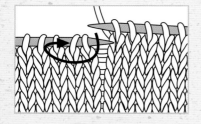

Knit 3 Together
(abbreviated K3 tog)

Insert the right needle into the **front** of the first three stitches on the left needle as if to **knit** (*Fig. 13*), then **knit** them together as if they were one stitch.

Fig. 13

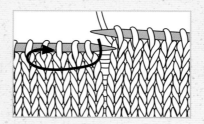

Purl 2 Together
(abbreviated P2 tog)

Insert the right needle into the **front** of the first two stitches on the left needle as if to **purl** (*Fig. 14*), then **purl** them together.

Fig. 14

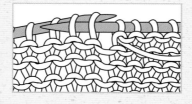

Purl 3 Together
(abbreviated P3 tog)

Insert the right needle into the **front** of the first three stitches on the left needle as if to **purl** (*Fig. 15*), then **purl** them together.

Fig. 15

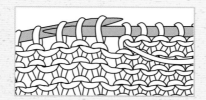

Slip, Slip, Knit
(abbreviated SSK)

Separately slip two stitches as if to **knit** (*Fig. 16a*). Insert the left needle into the **front** of both slipped stitches (*Fig. 16b*) and knit them together (*Fig. 16c*).

Fig. 16a

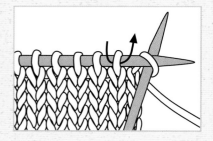

Fig. 16b

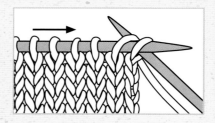

Fig. 16c

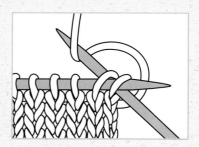

Slip, Slip, Purl
(abbreviated SSP)

Separately slip two stitches as if to **knit**. Place these two stitches **back** onto the left needle. Insert the right needle into the **back** of both stitches from **back** to **front** (*Fig. 17*) and purl them together.

Fig. 17

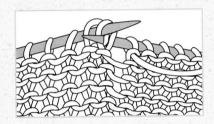

Slip 1, Knit 1, Pass Slipped Stitch Over
(abbreviated slip 1, K1, PSSO)

Slip one stitch as if to **knit**. Knit the next stitch. With the left needle, bring the slipped stitch over the knit stitch (*Fig. 18*) and off the needle.

Fig. 18

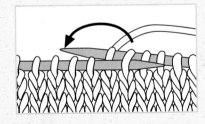

Slip 2 Together, Knit 1, Pass 2 Slipped Stitches Over
(abbreviated slip 2 sts tog, K1, P2SSO)

With yarn in back, slip two stitches together as if to **knit** (*Fig. 19a*), then knit the next stitch. With the left needle, bring the two slipped stitches over the stitch just made (*Fig. 19b*) and off the needle.

Fig. 19a

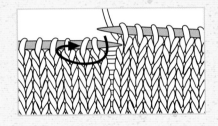

Fig. 19b

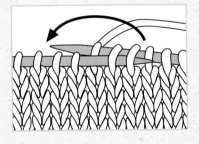

Picking Up Stitches

When instructed to pick up stitches, insert the needle from the **front** to the **back** under two strands at the edge of the worked piece (*Figs. 20a & b*). Put the yarn around the needle as if to **knit**, then bring the needle with the yarn back through the stitch to the right side, resulting in a stitch on the needle.

Repeat this along the edge, picking up the required number of stitches. A crochet hook may be helpful to pull yarn through.

Fig. 20a

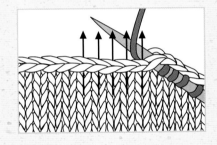

Fig. 20b

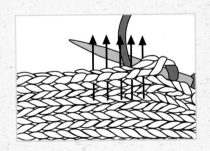

Weaving Seams

With the **right** side of both pieces facing you and edges even, sew through both sides once to secure the seam. Insert the needle under the bar **between** the first and second stitches on the row and pull the yarn through **(Fig. 21)**. Insert the needle under the next bar on the second side. Repeat from side to side, being careful to match rows. If the edges are different lengths, it may be necessary to insert the needle under two bars at one edge.

Fig. 21

Duplicate Stitch

Thread a yarn needle with an 18" (45.5 cm) length of yarn. With **right** side facing, bring the needle up from the wrong side at the base of the V, leaving an end to be woven in later (never tie knots). The needle should always go **between** the strands of yarn. Follow the right side of the V up and insert the needle from right to left under the legs of the V immediately above it, keeping the yarn on top of the stitch **(Fig. 22a)**, and draw through. Follow the left side of the V back down to the base and insert the needle back through the bottom of the same stitch where the first stitch began **(Fig. 22b, Duplicate Stitch completed)**.

Fig. 22a

Fig. 22b

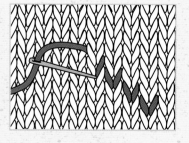

YARN INFORMATION

Projects in this leaflet were made using either Light Weight or Medium Weight Yarn. Any brand of the specified weight of yarn may be used. It is best to refer to the yardage/meters when determining how many balls or skeins to purchase. Remember, to arrive at the finished size, it is the GAUGE/TENSION that is important, not the brand of yarn.

For your convenience, listed below are the specific yarns used to create our photography models.

Barn Washcloth
Lion Brand® Lion® Cotton
#112 Poppy Red

Tractor Washcloth
Lion Brand® Lion® Cotton
#157 Sunflower

Tree Washcloth
Lily® Sugar'n Cream®
Green - #01712 Hot Green
Red - #01530 Country Red

Blanket
Lion Brand® Cupcake®
#106 Blueberry

Booties
Caron® Country
Brown - #0023 Chocolate Truffle
Coral - #0002 Coral Lipstick

Cardigan
Bernat® Softee® Baby
MC - #31307 Rock-A-Bye Baby
CC- #02000 White

Striped Hat
Caron® Country
Yellow - #0003 Soft Sunshine
Purple - #0006 Berry Frappe
Rose - #0001 Rose Bisque
Dk Purple - #0014 Deep Purple
Green - #0004 Green Sheen

Eyelet Cap
Lion Brand® Babysoft®
#141 Pink Lemonade

Blanket with Pig Hood
Bernat® Cottontots™
Pink - #90420 Pretty in Pink
Rose - #90421 Strawberry

Blanket with Chick Hood
Bernat® Cottontots™
Yellow - #90615 Sunshine
Bright Yellow - #90616 Lemon Berry
Rose - #90421 Strawberry

Piggie
TLC® Cotton Plus™
Pink - #3706 Light Rose
Rose - #3707 Medium Rose
Black - #3002 Black

Cow
TLC® Cotton Plus™
Black - #3002 Black
White - #3001 White
Pink - #3706 Light Rose

Credits

Production Team:
Instructional Editor - Sarah J. Green
Technical Editor - Lois J. Long
Editorial Writer - Susan McManus Johnson
Senior Graphic Artist - Lora Puls
Lead Graphic Artist - Angela Ormsby Stark
Graphic Artist - Jacob Casleton
Production Artist - Janie Marie Wright
Photo Stylists - Christy Myers and Sondra Daniel
Photographers - Mark Matthews and Ken West

We have made every effort to ensure that these instructions are accurate and complete. We cannot, however, be responsible for human error, typographical mistakes or variations in individual work.

Items made and instructions tested by Sue Galucki, Freda Gillham, Raymelle Greening, Dale Potter and Margaret Taverner.